AF481418

Hex codes, or hexadecimal codes, are a way to represent colors in digital devices and web design. Each hex code refers to a very specific color. A hex color is expressed as a six-digit combination of numbers and letters, preceded by a pound sign or hashtag, defined by its mix of red, green, and blue (RGB). The first two letters or numbers refer to red, the next two refer to green, and the last two refer to blue.

The color values are defined as values between 00 and FF. Hex codes are a universal way to describe colors. This book is specifically about shades of orange.

A is for alloy orange

A

#C46210

a is for atomic tangerine

a

#FF9966

B is for bittersweet

B

#FE6F5E

b is for burnt orange

b

#CC5500

C is for cheese orange

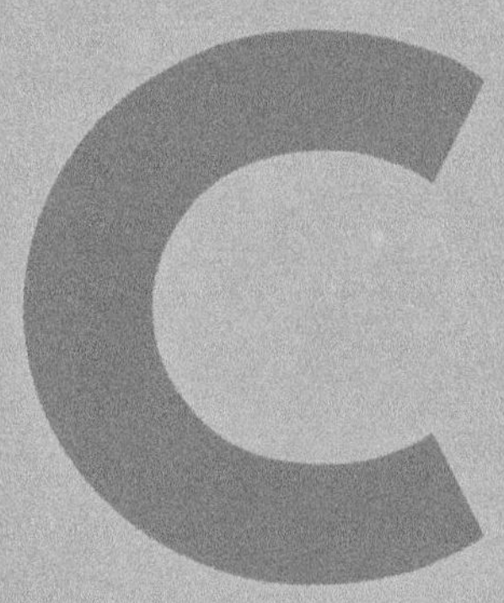

#FFA600

c is for chocolate orange

c

#D2691E

D is for desert orange

#ED8E4A

d is for dragon fire
orange

d

#FD652D

E is for ecstasy

E

#FA7814

e is for euxanth

e

#E3A857

F is for flamenco

F

#FF7D07

f is for flamingo

#F2552A

G is for gold drop

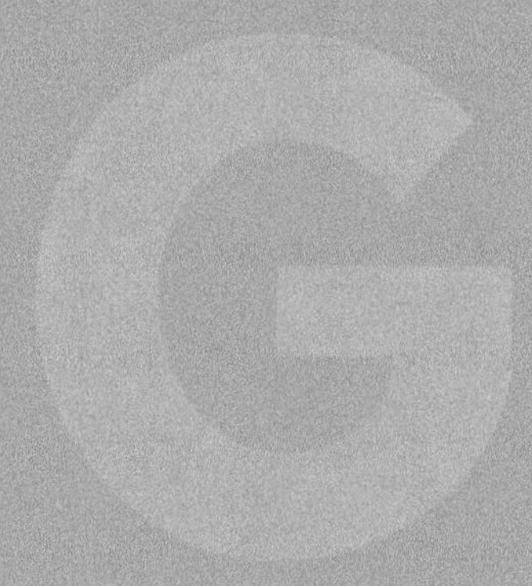

#F18200

g is for goldfish

g

#FF9913

J is for jack-o-lantern orange

#F4781E

j is for jaguar

j

#F6861D

K is for kanzo-iro

K

#FF8936

k is for kincha

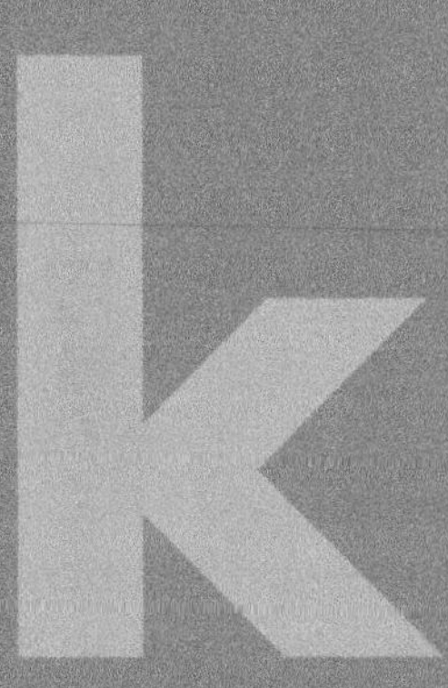

#C66B27

L is for lead tetroxide

L

#F95810

l is for light apricot

#FDD5B1

M is for marigold orange

M

#EAA221

m is for mimosa orange

m

#FFCA4B

N is for neon carrot

N

#FFA343

n is for neon tangerine

n

#F6890A

O is for orange spice

#D76B00

o is for outrageous orange

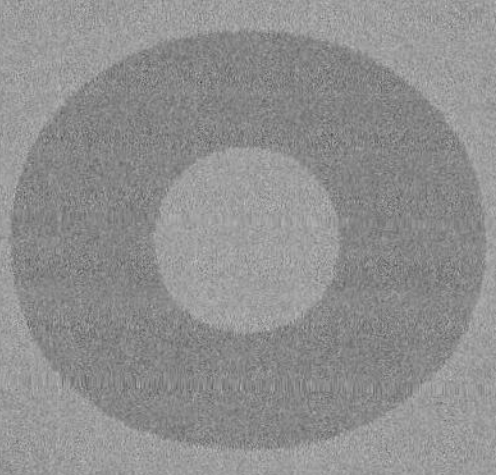

#FF6E4A

P is for peach orange

P

#FFCC99

p is for pumpkin orange

p

#FF7518

Q is for quilted bag

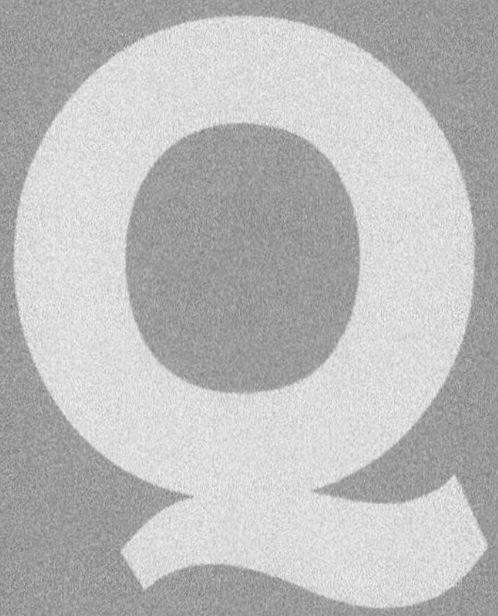

#D29565

q is for quince gold

q

#F6CC86

R is for rajah

R

#FBAB60

r is for rare sausage

r

#F88B30

s is for salamander

orange

#F05E23

T is for tamarillo orange

#FE8915

t is for tango

#ED7A1C

W is for web orange

W

#FFA500

w is for willpower

orange

w

#FD5602

X is for x23 apricot

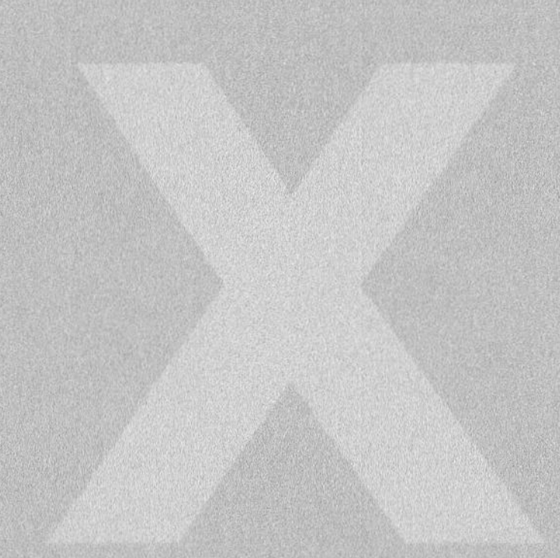

#FEB36F

x is for xanthous 2

#FBC973

Y is for yams

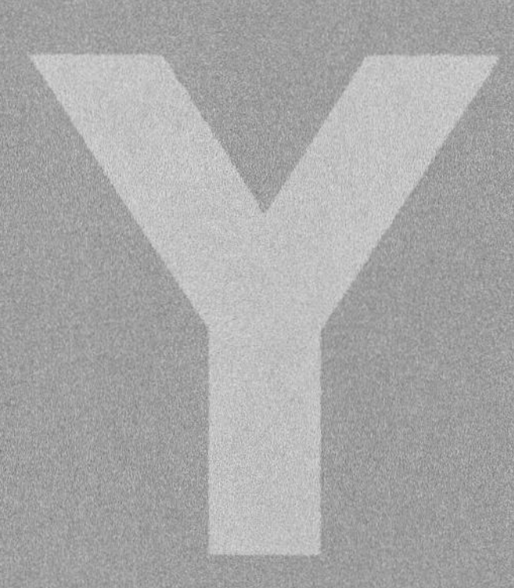

#E08A4F

y is for yellow sea

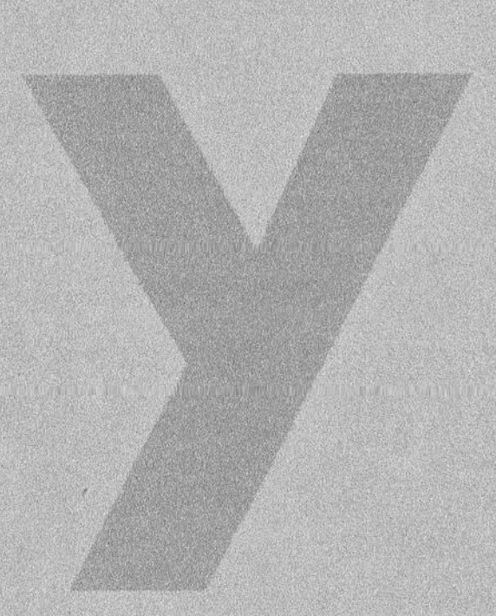

#FEA904

Z is for zambia

Z

#FF9215

z is for zest

z

#E5841B

www.ingramcontent.com/pod-product-compliance
Lightning Source LLC
Chambersburg PA
CBHW040153110726
48005CB00018B/2744